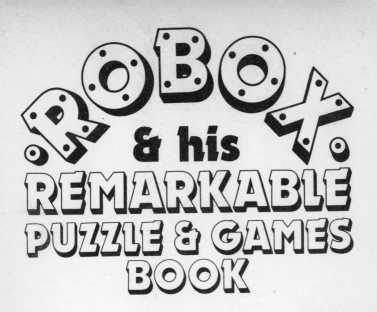

ROBOX & his REMARKABLE PUZZLE & GAMES BOOK

A Beaver Book
Published by Arrow Books Limited
62–5 Chandos Place, London WC2N 4NW

An imprint of Century Hutchinson Ltd

London Melbourne Sydney Auckland
Johannesburg and agencies throughout the world

First published 1988
© Naomi Games 1988

This book is sold subject to the condition that it shall not, by way of trade or otherwise, be lent, resold, hired out, or otherwise circulated without the publisher's prior consent in any form of binding or cover other than that in which it is published and without a similar condition including this condition being imposed on the subsequent purchaser.

Set in Times
by JH Graphics Ltd, Reading

Made and printed in Great Britain
by The Guernsey Press Co. Ltd.,
Guernsey, C.I.

ISBN 0 09 956760 1

For Timothy and Katherine, with love

ROBOX & his REMARKABLE PUZZLE & GAMES BOOK

Naomi Games

Beaver Books

CONTENTS

INTRODUCTION	**6**
HOW TO . . .	**8**
KEY TO SYMBOLS	**10**
1. CREATE COMPUTER CONTROL . . .	**11**

Special equipment: wool or string,
    4 paper-clips, 1 marble

2. MAKING FRIENDS	**22**
3. ENTER FIDOX	**39**

Special equipment: sweet wrappers or tin foil
    sticky stars
    coins (optional)

4. ROBOX ROCKS AT THE ROXY	**49**

Special equipment: 2 lollipop sticks
    wool or string
    sticky stars
    30 buttons or beads (small)
    2 dice (optional)

5. DETECTIVE ROBOX TO THE RESCUE	**64**

Special equipment: sweet wrappers

6. A COSMIC CIRCUS COMES TO TOWN	**70**

Special equipment: 4 marbles, a torch
    sweet wrappers
    buttons or beads (15–25)

7. ROBOX ROCKETS AROUND THE WORLD	**84**

Special equipment: sweet wrappers
    a glass of water

8. ROBOX FINDS THE ANSWERS	**92**

YOU WILL NEED...

Everything listed below is available at most large stationers, but have a look at home first to see what you already have.

Essential Equipment
If you are going to make Robox and friends, you will need **all** these things **throughout** this book:

- A3 size, thick, cartridge pad of paper (if you can find thick, centimetre graph paper, great!)
- Compass, for drawing circles
- Double-sided tape (this is best) or a good glue stick
- Adhesive tape
- Pencils, coloured crayons, coloured pencils or felt-tip pens
- Centimetre ruler (as long as possible)
- Scissors – **careful**, not too sharp
- String and wool
- Gummed stars and shapes for decoration
- Tin foil
- Coloured **transparent** cellophane (you can use sweet wrappers)
- Split pins, also called paper fasteners:

  — head
  — tail
  Split pin

Not essential but will come in handy
- Tracing or greaseproof paper
- Set square   • Pin   • Empty ballpoint pen
- Rubber   • Scrap paper
- Masking tape, for positioning flaps, sides, etc., before sticking down
- Craft knife, to make slits in paper. You **MUST** ask an adult to help you and show you how to use it.
- Access to a photocopying machine

- See page 4 for special equipment needed for each chapter.

INTRODUCTION

All the projects are easy to do – just follow the instructions and work carefully. It is best to start with the first project and work through the book. Once you've mastered making a box and cutting slits, etc., you will be able to take on **anything**!

Please read pages 4–10 and all instructions carefully. **Be cool** and **careful**! Try not to write in this book or cut it up.

You don't have to make Robox and friends, you can just do the puzzles and games on your own or with friends, but you will have more fun if you make the characters. **Always** ask a grown-up to help you if you get stuck, and ask them to show you how to use the tools you need.

This book should keep you amused for ages. Once you've made Robox and his friends, you can keep them safely in a box and play with them whenever you wish. You can make lots of Roboxes, more disguises, and invent your own characters. Colour, decorate and draw the faces of Robox and friends as you wish, but **enjoy** yourself whilst making and doing.

Most of the things to make in this book are based on a **GRID**, which is a pattern of squares to guide you. It is easy to follow once you know how.

Spend some time before beginning this book making your own grids, covering lots of sheets of square, A3 size, thick, cartridge paper with 1 centimetre (cm) squares. Number the squares along the top, bottom and down the sides. This will help you follow the shape (pattern) on the grid. Rule the grid lines in pencil and use a thicker, darker pencil to draw the shape you need. See page 8 for further instructions. Always write the letters and numbers on the flaps and sides as shown in the book, on **YOUR** grid shape to help you follow the instructions.

In some cases, if you feel confident enough, you needn't draw all the grid lines, but just measure your centimetres with a ruler. Always use cartridge paper, because it is thick and strong.

All the grids in this book are shown half size. The numbers around the edges represent squares of 1 centimetre (cm), so **remember** to draw 1 centimetre squares on your grids so that Robox and friends will be twice as big as shown in the book!

| 1 | 2 | 3 | 4 | 5 | 6 | 7 | 8 | 9cm |

centimetre (cm) measure – exact size

Remember:
- **Always** ask a grown-up to help you.
- **Always** ask a grown-up to show you how to cut slits, etc., and how to use tools.
- **Never** cut through paper on to a table.
- Always put thick card under the surface you need to cut.

HOW TO...

1. Draw a grid: Using a pencil and ruler on A3 size, thick, cartridge paper, mark 1cm intervals on all 4 sides of the paper. Using your ruler to guide you, join up the marks as shown. ▶

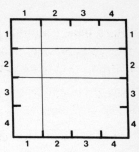

2. Plot with a dot! When copying a shape on to a grid, read the numbers of the squares needed to make your shape and mark your grid with small dots. Join up the dots with a heavy line to make the shape you need. ▶

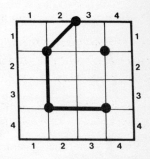

3. Fold: Place a ruler along the fold line, holding firmly down with one hand, and run the point of a sharp pencil, empty ballpoint pen or your fingernail down the fold line to 'score' the line. Keeping the ruler in place, lift the side of the paper towards the ruler's edge and run your thumb nail along the fold line to make a crisp fold.

4. Cut out a shape: Carefully use scissors to cut along cut line: ─────────

5. Make a hole: Carefully pierce the centre with a pin, compass point or sharp pencil. Then use a ballpoint pen or sharp pencil point to make the hole bigger.

6. Cut out a circle: Pierce a hole in the centre of the circle, then cut to the edge and around the cut line.

7. Cut a slit: Start at the centre of the slit, piercing a hole first, then cut along slit line.

8. Use glue: Don't use too much! Read instructions.

9. Use double-sided tape: This is best for sticking flaps. Apply to grid surface, trim around shape and peel off the backing **only** when you are ready to stick down flaps.

10. Use masking tape: Little pieces will hold the sides in position before sticking firmly. Then peel off, **carefully**.

11. Find the centre of a square: Lightly draw 2 diagonal lines from the corners of your square. The centre will be the point at which they meet.

12. Trace: Hold the page you want to trace against a window, cover with cartridge paper, then draw around image. Or just cover with tracing or greaseproof paper and draw around image.

A KEY TO SYMBOLS

———	Cut along line
- - - - -	Fold along line
—·—·—	Position paper on this line
●—·—·—●	Position corners on circles
■———■	Cut slit from ■ to ■
┤———■	Cut slit from edge to ■
(trapezoid with dashes)	Stick flap
●	Make hole
Base	bottom
(square with ⊗)	Centre of square or circle (place compass point here)
(square with ●)	Make hole at centre of square or circle
(grey square)	Cut inside this shape
(dotted or grey square)	Draw this shape
·····•·····	Draw shape but do not cut
(two grids with arrows)	Grid sides together

Radius (page 76) – Distance from centre to outside edge of circle.

··CREATE·· ··COMPUTER·· ··CONTROL··

Hello, I'm Mission Mouse. I scamper around this book enjoying myself and squeaking instructions. Here is your first mission . . .

Create Computer Control, the home and heart of our hero, Robox. When you've made it, attach it to the inside front cover and title page of this book, with 4 paper-clips so that it pops up whenever you need it. When you have made Robox, join him to Computer Control at hole **1**, with wool or thin string (about 65cm). Robox will sit by you whilst you are using this book and sit ON it when you are not!

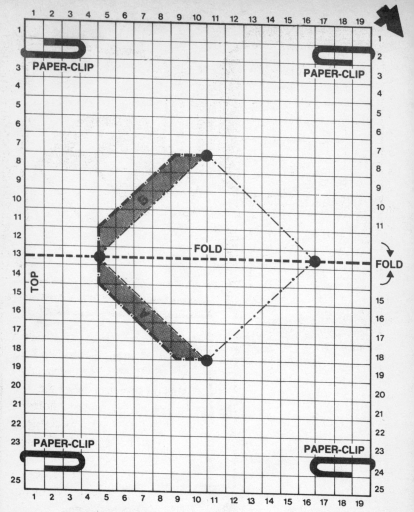

The Computer Control base

Cut a rectangle of cartridge paper, 25cm by 19cm. Draw the grid in pencil as shown. Mark 4 big dots to indicate where to lay the 4 corners of the computer. The diamond shape in the centre shows where to place it. Fold the paper in half, grid sides together.

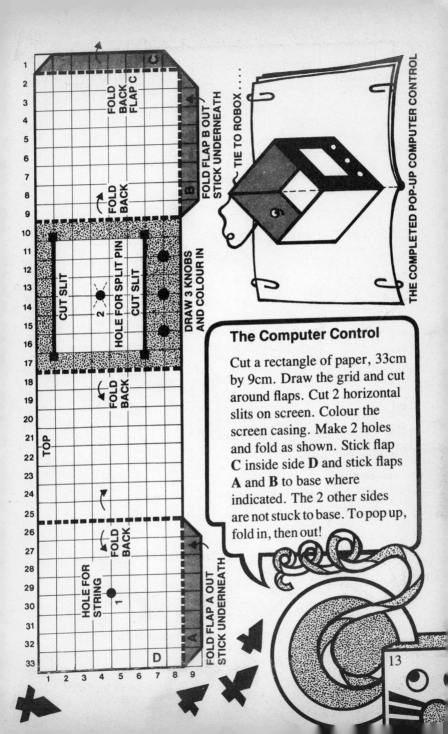

THE COMPLETED POP-UP COMPUTER CONTROL

The Computer Control

Cut a rectangle of paper, 33cm by 9cm. Draw the grid and cut around flaps. Cut 2 horizontal slits on screen. Colour the screen casing. Make 2 holes and fold as shown. Stick flap **C** inside side **D** and stick flaps **A** and **B** to base where indicated. The 2 other sides are not stuck to base. To pop up, fold in, then out!

Who do I belong to?

Photocopy or copy this 8cm by 6cm label and cut it out. Fill in your name. Starting at the back of the top slit of Computer Control, thread the label over the screen then back behind the knobs you have drawn at the bottom. Oh, dear, is there, or is there not, a knot in my tail? Use some string and find out! SQUEAK!

Answer: page 92

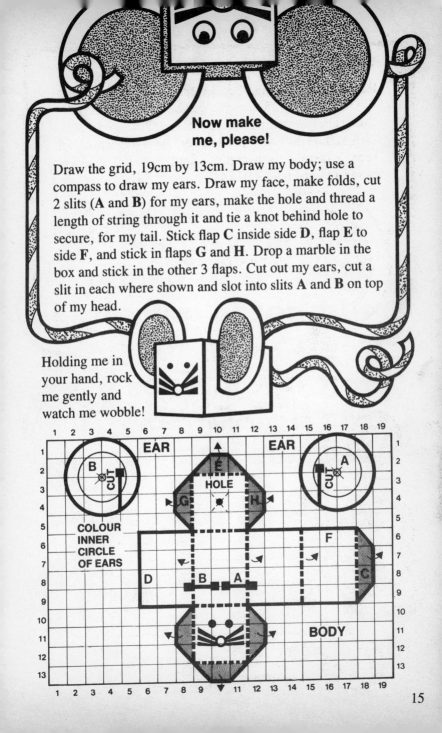

Now make me, please!

Draw the grid, 19cm by 13cm. Draw my body; use a compass to draw my ears. Draw my face, make folds, cut 2 slits (**A** and **B**) for my ears, make the hole and thread a length of string through it and tie a knot behind hole to secure, for my tail. Stick flap **C** inside side **D**, flap **E** to side **F**, and stick in flaps **G** and **H**. Drop a marble in the box and stick in the other 3 flaps. Cut out my ears, cut a slit in each where shown and slot into slits **A** and **B** on top of my head.

Holding me in your hand, rock me gently and watch me wobble!

A RIDDLE

My 1st is in three
But not in ten.
My 2nd is in two
And also in one.
My 3rd is in billion
But not in million.
My 4th is in four
But not in five.
My 5th is in six
But not in seven.

And so I ask you,

Who am I?

Answer: page 92

Follow these instructions:

Hello, I'm your hero, Robox! To make me come to life, draw the 2 grids, each 20cm by 28cm, and copy the patterns overleaf. Draw my face, cut out all the pieces, cut the slits and make all the holes. Make all the folds (downwards) but do not fold the eye strip yet. Carefully cut out the 2 square eye holes on my head. Now assemble me, but keep looking at me on page 29 for guidance:

1. With grid sides facing, attach a split pin through my head and body at hole **A**.

INSTRUCTIONS CONTINUED▶

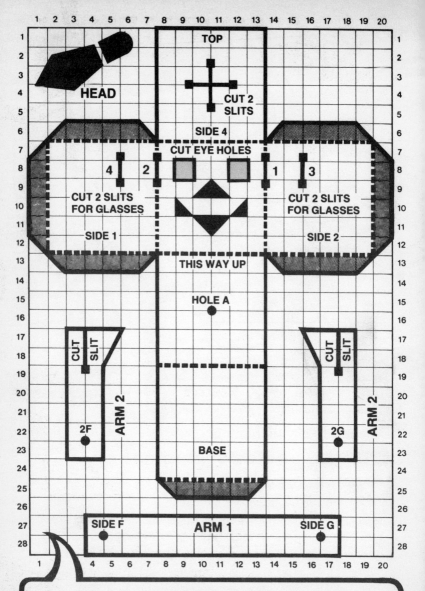

2. Fold down sides **1** and **2** of **body**. Stick flaps **J** inside side **3**. Stick flaps **L** inside side **4**.

3. Thread arm **1**, starting with side **F**, into slit **G**, through my **body** and out at slit **F**.

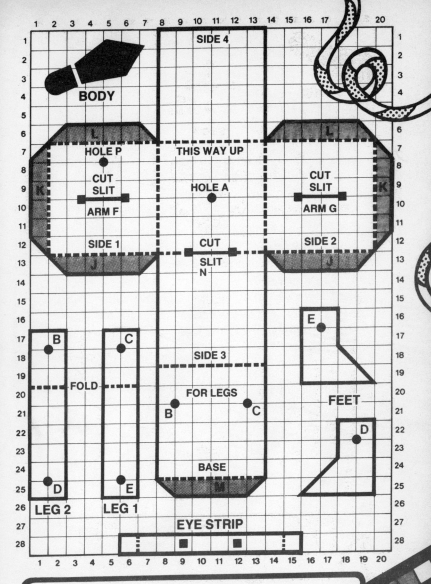

4. Attach arm piece **2F** to side **F** of arm **1** and piece **2G** to side **G**, with a split pin each.

5. Attach me with a piece of string to my Computer Control through hole **P**.

CONTINUED ▶

The making of me, continued:

Tie a knot **inside** my body to secure one end and pass the other end through hole **1** of Computer, tying another knot **inside** the Computer Control.

6. With grid sides together, attach leg **1**, hole **C**, to hole **C** on base of body with a split pin. Attach leg **2**, hole **B** to hole **B** on base of body, with a split pin. The tails of the pins should be **inside** my body. With 2 split pins attach foot **E** to hole **E** on my leg and foot **D** to hole **D**.

7. Stick flap **M** of base to side **4** and stick flaps **K** inside the sides of the base to make a box.

8. Now to my head: Thread the eye strip into slit **1**, **behind** my face and out at slit **2**. Make the 2 folds on either side to secure.

9. Fold down the top of my head and stick all the flaps into the sides of my head to make a box. Stick the top and bottom flaps down first. Now I am ready for action! Thank you!

Robox, the Crossword King!

Draw a grid, 6cm by 6cm and copy the crossword on page 21. Write your answers on your grid or on a side of Robox! All the 8 clues are somewhere on these 2 pages.

MAKING FRIENDS 2

Mission... Test your memory...

O.K! Before we make friends, let's test your memory! Make as many cards, 8cm by 6cm, as you like. I suggest no more than 12. (See label on page 14 for size.) With a friend, draw a simple picture, a number or a letter on each. Slot the cards one by one into my screen, or turn them face up on a table. When you've seen them all, put them away. Then test your memory by trying to draw all of them – in any order. When you've finished, check and see how well you've done. Now look at the 8 cards on page 23 for a few minutes, then draw them without looking!

> Please, Computer Control, may I have some friends to share these pages with?

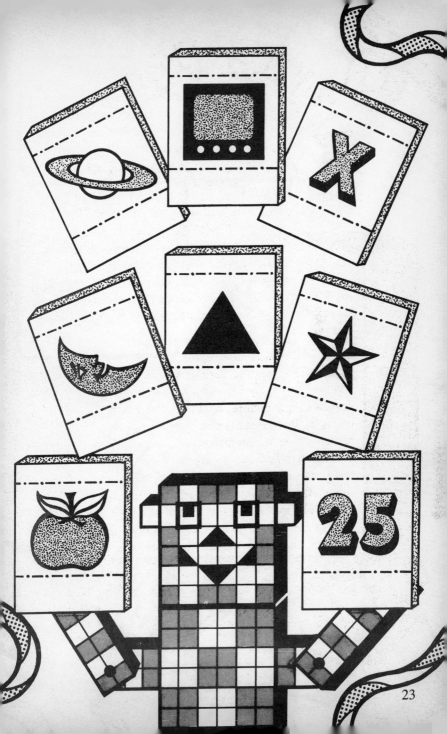

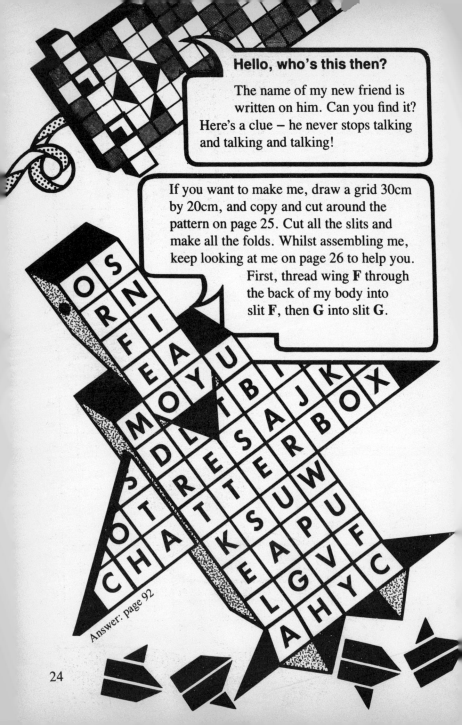

Hello, who's this then?

The name of my new friend is written on him. Can you find it? Here's a clue – he never stops talking and talking and talking!

If you want to make me, draw a grid 30cm by 20cm, and copy and cut around the pattern on page 25. Cut all the slits and make all the folds. Whilst assembling me, keep looking at me on page 26 to help you.

First, thread wing **F** through the back of my body into slit **F**, then **G** into slit **G**.

Answer: page 92

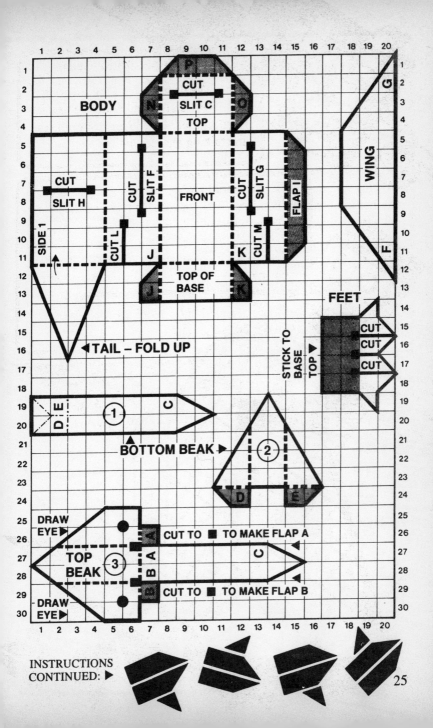

Stick flap **I** to side **1**. Stick my feet to my base, stick flap **J** to side **J** and flap **K** to side **K**.

Now make my beak:

Bottom beak: Position pieces **1** and **2** (piece **2** being the wrong way up) as shown below. Stick flap **D** to side **D** and, folding beak up and to the right, stick flap **E** to side **E**.

Top beak: Position piece **3** as shown below and stick flap **A** to side **A** and flap **B** to side **B**. Now, holding the top beak in one hand, push the bottom beak up into it, as in diagram below.

Holding the 2 long strips of the beak together, slot points **C** into the front of slit **C**, at the top of my body, push through, into my body, and out again through slit **H**.

Then stick the flaps on top of my body down to the sides of my body.

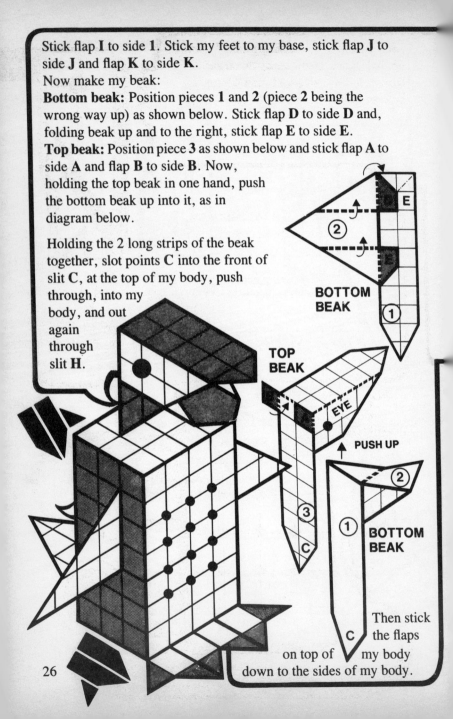

Make me talk, by pushing point **C** gently up and down! I will sit on the arm of Robox if you slot slits **L** and **M** into his arm as shown on page 29!

Dotty Puzzles

Try these! If you like, draw the 12 dots on my body or copy the grid below.

1. Using 8 straight lines and without taking your pencil off the paper, try to join up all the dots.
2. Then try to join up all the 12 dots with 5 straight lines, again without lifting your pencil off the paper. Think very hard!

The grid measures 7cm by 4cm.

Answer: page 92

Games to play all over Robox!

Play these games **on** Robox or on a grid 6cm by 6cm.

1. How many squares can you make using this grid? Careful! **Or** — you can just colour in all the squares on Robox!

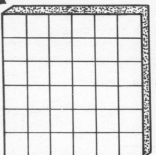

2. Here's a game to play with a friend. Each choose a different coloured pencil. Take turns to draw a line along a side of a square. The aims are to make as many boxes as possible and stop your friend from making boxes. Write your initial in each box you make. The one who makes the most, wins!

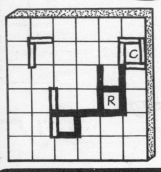

3. Write a sentence in the squares, with the letters in the correct order. Start in any square and go in any direction, across, down or diagonally, left or right. Fill in the rest of the squares with any other letters. Tell your friend the letter the sentence begins with and ask him to find it. This sentence begins with **H**!

H	Y	C	X	S	K
E	B	M	Y	N	F
L	L	O	H	A	J
Q	O	B	O	M	E
W	X	D	R	I	T
M	O	Z	S	R	A

Answer: page 92

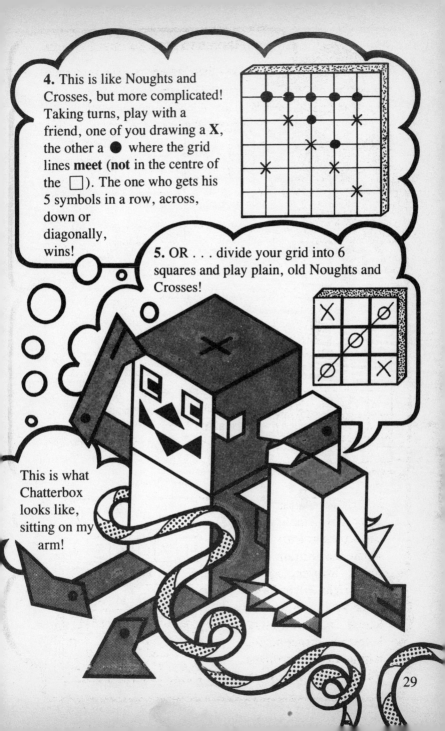

A word game to play with a friend

Cut out 26 cards from a grid, 6cm by 8cm. (Look at page 14 for guidance.) Write one letter of the alphabet on each. Shuffle the pack, ask a friend to choose a card at random and slot it into my computer screen. Write the chosen letter anywhere on **ME** or on a grid with

Someone has been playing on me! Can you find 28 words of 3 or more letters hidden on me?

Answer: page 93

as many squares as you like. Put the card back in the pack, shuffle again, taking turns to choose a letter and write it on me or on your grid. Each time, try to make as many words, across, down or diagonally as you can. See how many words of 3 or more letters you can make. You may count a word within a word, e.g: Robox=2, bookworm=3 words.

Colourvision

Draw a grid, 6cm by 8cm. Copy the letter A below. Colour the background red and the central ▲ black. Slot it into my screen. Stare at the ▲ for 25 seconds, then look quickly at a piece of white paper. What magic happens?

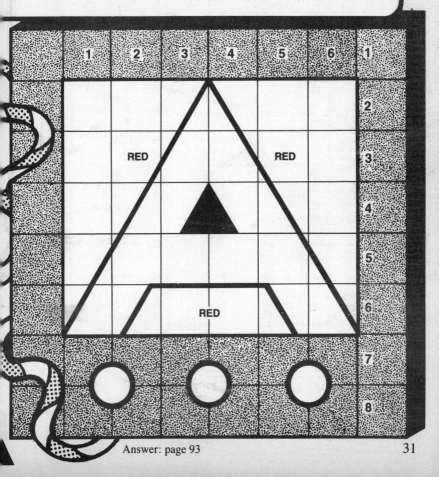

Answer: page 93

Make a Tangram

The tangram is an ancient Chinese puzzle, a bit like a jigsaw. Copy this square grid, 8cm by 8cm. Divide it into 16 squares. Cut along the heavy lines to make 7 pieces. See how many different pictures you can make just by using your 7 pieces of paper. Magic!

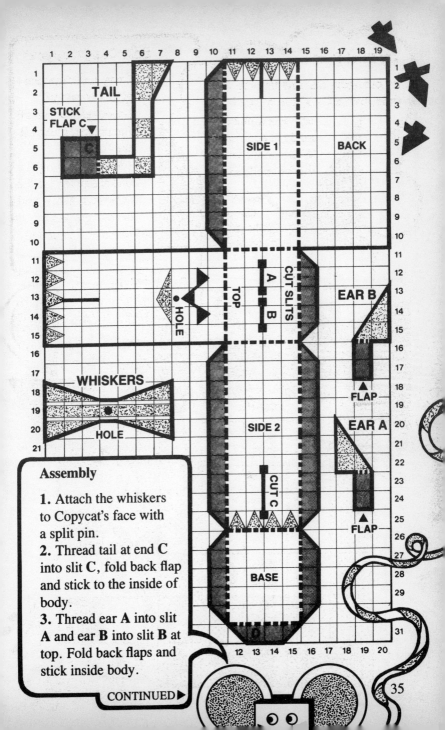

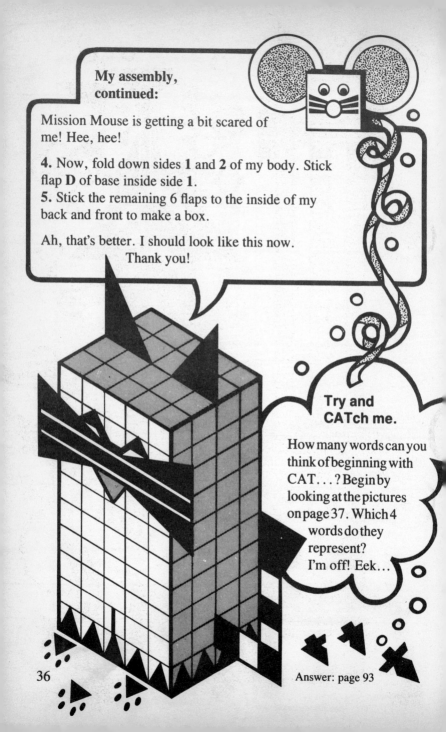

Eek! Help!

START

The tail's end!

Miaow! Be nice and guide me with your finger to the end of Mission Mouse's tail! Miaow!

Uh! Squeak, squeak . . . no thanks to you, I survived to tell my 'tail'. I was rescued just in time by a Mission Mouse's best friend – the faithful FIDOX! If you want to make him, turn over . . .

Guessing Game

Without counting first, guess how many spots you can see on Fidox. No cheating! Eek, eek . . .

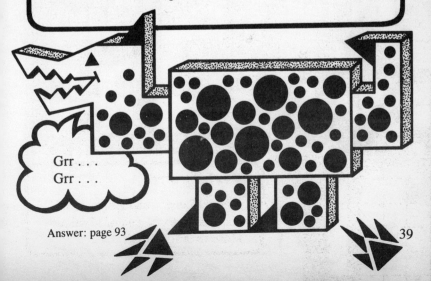

Answer: page 93

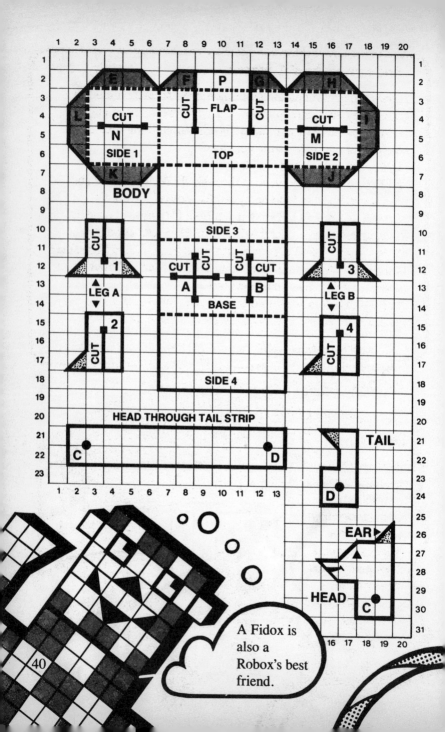

And now make ME, please . . .

Draw the grid, copy the pattern on page 40 and colour the tips of my ears, tail and feet. Cut all the slits, make all the folds (downwards) and holes. Whilst assembling me, keep looking at me, below, for guidance.

1. Stick flaps **K** and **J** to side **3**.
2. Thread head and tail strip through slit **M**, into body and out at slit **N**. Hole **D** to be by slit **M**, hole **C** by slit **N**.
3. With a split pin, attach head at hole **C** to hole **C** on strip.
4. With a split pin, attach tail at hole **D** to hole **D** on strip.
5. Stick flaps **I** and **L** to base and flaps **E**, **F**, **G** and **H** to side **4** to make a box. Tuck in the flap **P** on my top, without sticking, so you can open the box!
6. Leg **A**: Slot piece **2** into piece **1** then slot the 2 joined pieces into the cross-slits on the base. Repeat with leg **B**.

Before putting me together, cover me with spots, then assemble me and ask your friends to guess how many spots I have on me!

Lucky Dip

With eyes closed, take turns with a friend to score a point, but **only** if your finger lands on a number. Score 2 points if you land on a ●. Keep score. The first one to reach 50 wins!

Come on, Fidox . . .

Cut a piece of cartridge paper, 19cm by 4cm. Stand one 19cm side, upright along the dotted line. Slowly, lower your head and look closely at Fidox with your left eye. You should see him walk towards me! Now turn this book sideways and try to join up our broken lead. No drawing the missing piece – use your eyes only! Tricky!

Here are some problems to solve with 10 discs or coins. When you've finished, you can store the discs inside your Fidox Box.

1. You need 10 discs or coins. Arrange 10 discs in 5 straight lines, with 4 discs in each line.

2. You need 6 discs or coins. Arrange them like this:

Try, in 3 moves only, to form a circle of discs or coins. Move only one at a time. It should always be touching 2 others at the end of the move.

3. You need 8 discs (4 coloured, 4 white) or 8 coins (4 copper, 4 silver). Draw a grid, 30cm by 3cm. Divide into 10 like this:

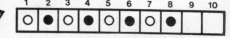

Moving 2 at a time, in 4 moves only try to arrange the 4 coloured discs (copper coins) in a row, with the 4 white (silver) ones next to them.

Answer: page 93

O.K. I'm bored! Let's liven things up a bit and move and groove . . . Help me get my gear on, please, so let's . . . **Cut and run** . . .

1. Copy and draw the grid on page 47.
2. Cut out my 2 hair-pieces and colour them, back and front, in disgusting, bright colours!

3. Make slits and slot piece **1** into piece **2**. Then slot the 2 joined pieces into the cross-slits on top of my head. (You can see the slits on pages 18 and 29).

4. Cut out my glasses and cut out the 2 centre holes. Colour the frames. Cut out 2 pieces of coloured cellophane (sweet wrappers) or use tin foil to make the lenses. Stick to the back of the frames with adhesive tape.

5. Make the 4 folds. Slot flap **A** into slit **4** on my head; then slot flap **B** into slit **3** on my head. Refer to page 18.

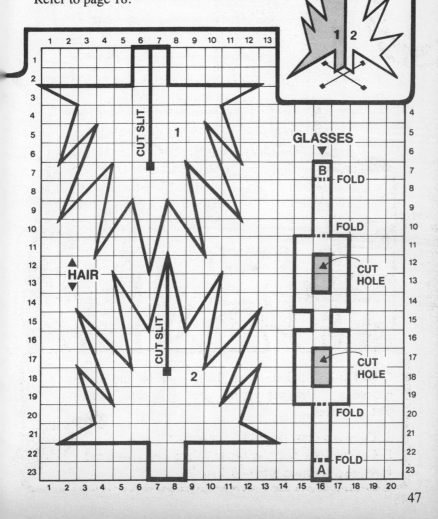

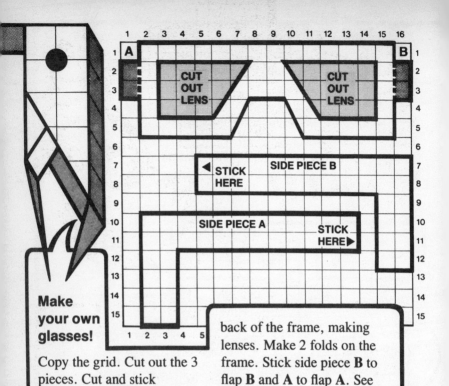

Make your own glasses!

Copy the grid. Cut out the 3 pieces. Cut and stick coloured cellophane to the back of the frame, making lenses. Make 2 folds on the frame. Stick side piece **B** to flap **B** and **A** to flap **A**. See how weird everything looks!

Answer: page 94

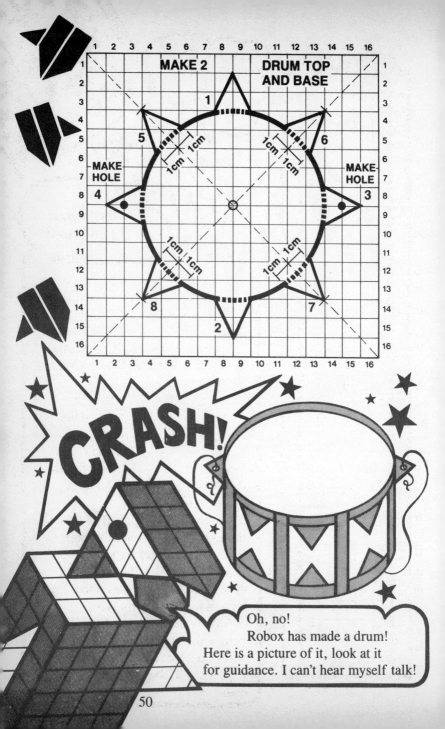

Beat your drum with 2 lollipop sticks.

Make your own drum!

1. Top and base: Follow the grid on page 50. Use a compass. Make 8 flaps. For flaps **5** to **8**, divide the square diagonally as shown, then measure 1cm on either side of the divisions to give the position of flaps. Cut out the top, lay it on a sheet of paper, draw round it and cut a second shape for the base. Make 2 holes on the drum **top** only.

2. Sides: Copy, colour and cut out the grid on this page. Make 8 slits on both sides. Bend back flap **A** and stick to side **B**.

3. Assembly: Slot flaps **1–8** of top through the 8 slits on drum side. Fold over and stick down all but flaps **3** and **4**. Slot, fold and stick down flaps **1–8** of base on the bottom 8 slits of drum side.

4. Measure enough wool (from your waist to the back of your neck, doubled) and thread through flaps **3** and **4**. Tie a knot at both ends.

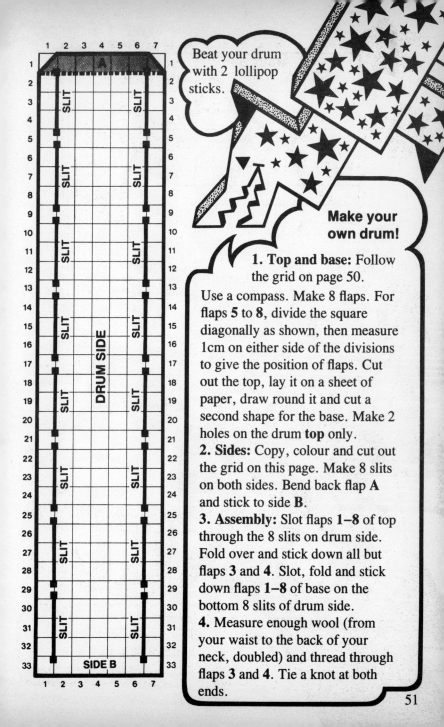

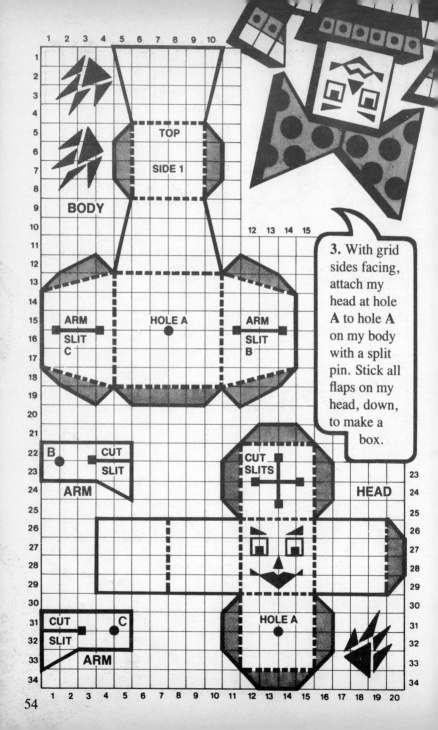

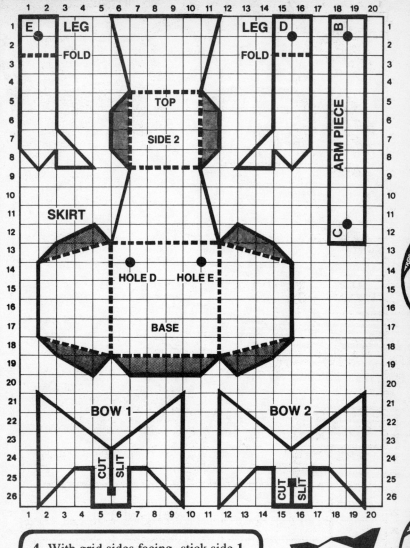

4. With grid sides facing, stick side **1** of her body to side **2** of her skirt.

5. Thread the arm piece, starting with side **B**, through, into slit **C** and out at slit **B**. Attach arm **B** to hole **B** with a split pin.

CONTINUED ▶

Make me, continued:

6. Attach my arm **C**, to hole **C** with a split pin.

7. With grid sides facing, attach leg **D** to hole **D** on my base with a split pin, repeat with leg **E**.

8. Stick all flaps down to make my body and stick all flaps down to make my skirt.

9. Draw a pattern on the 2 bow pieces. Make a slit in each, then slot piece **2** into piece **1** and slot them both into the top of my head. Thank you!

How about colouring me in some jazzy colours when you've made me?

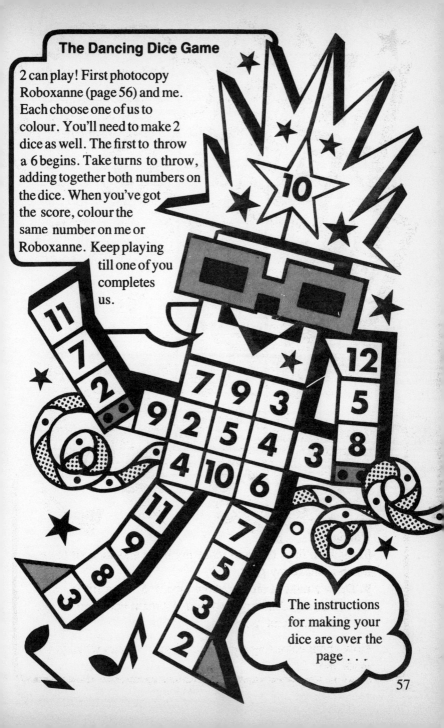

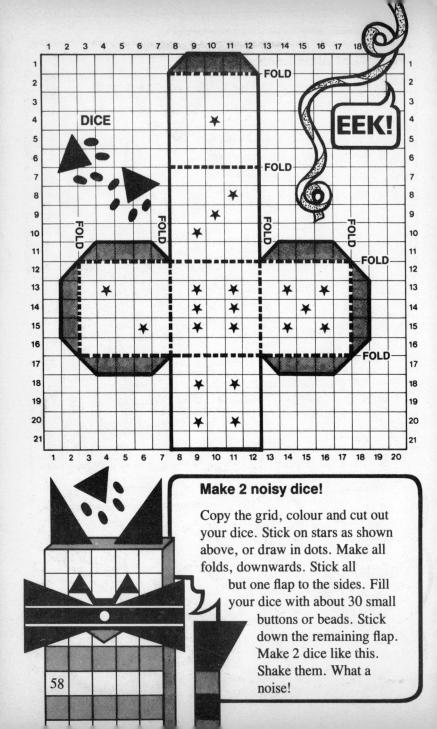

Make 2 noisy dice!

Copy the grid, colour and cut out your dice. Stick on stars as shown above, or draw in dots. Make all folds, downwards. Stick all but one flap to the sides. Fill your dice with about 30 small buttons or beads. Stick down the remaining flap. Make 2 dice like this. Shake them. What a noise!

Play the Robox Game

More than 2 can play. All the players need paper and pencil, and a copy of this list:

2 – Head	8 – Hands
3 – Body	9 – One eye
4 – Arms	10 – One eye
5 – Legs	11 – Nose
6 – Wig or hat	12 – Mouth
7 – Feet	

Each player is aiming to complete a drawing of Robox. Take turns to throw both dice. Add the numbers together. You can't begin until you get a '6'. Draw the bit of Robox which corresponds to the total you have thrown. The winner is the one who finishes Robox first!

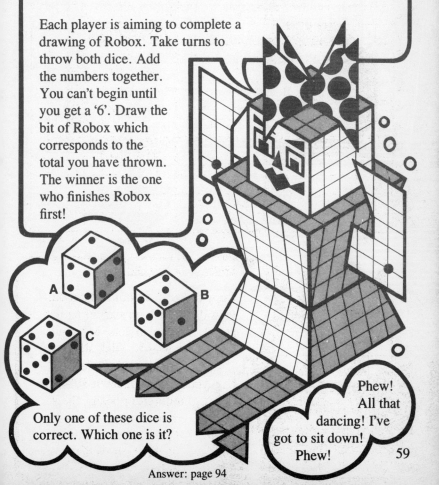

Only one of these dice is correct. Which one is it?

Phew! All that dancing! I've got to sit down! Phew!

Answer: page 94

Top 20

1. Jingle Bells
2. 10 Green Bottles
3. Twist and Shout
4. Yellow Submarine
5. La Bamba
6. Oranges and Lemons
7. Waltzing Matilda
8. Teddy Bears' Picnic
9. The Wizard of Oz
10. Old Macdonald
11. She Loves You
12. My Way
13. One More River
14. Bobby Shafto
15. 3 Blind Mice
16. Star Trekkin'
17. The Birthday Song
18. The Hokey Cokey
19. Help!
20. Love Me Tender

For 2 Players

Oldies, but Goodies!

A game to play: 1. Each player writes a list of his or her 20 favourite songs, as shown above. Then . . .

2. One of you draw a grid, 6cm by 8cm. Write the numbers 1 to 20 in the squares, and draw stars down the side as shown here. Slot this card into Computer Control. Then . . .

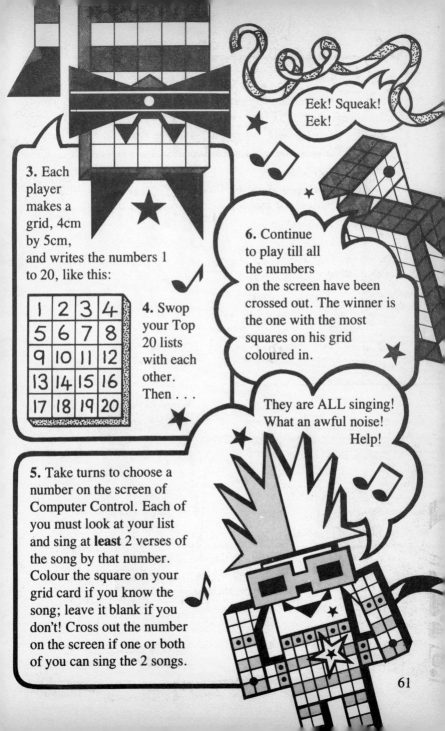

DETECTIVE ROBOX TO THE RESCUE

Fidox has run away . . . the search begins. But first . . .

I must don my Detective's Outfit . . .

1. **My glasses:** You've already made them on page 47.
2. Copy, colour and cut out the grid on page 65. Make all folds, slits and the hole on my magnifying glass (use a compass to draw this).
3. **My wig:** Make the 2 pieces, **A** and **B**. Slot piece **A** into piece **B** and slot both pieces into the 2 slits on top of my head.

CONTINUED ▶

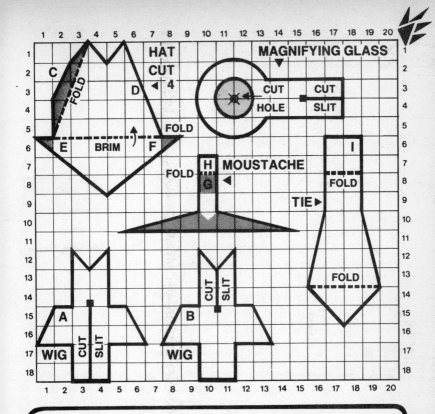

4. The hat: Cut out 4 identical pieces. Stick flap **C** of the first piece to side **D** of the second piece. Repeat with all 4 pieces, joining piece **4** to piece **1**, to make a 4-sided shape.

5. The moustache: Colour as shown. Colour square **G** the same colour as the glasses. Fold back square **H** and clip on to the glasses.

6. The tie: Make it snazzy! Tuck flap **I** into slit **N** on Robox's body (see page 19).

7. The magnifying glass: Cover the hole with a piece of sweet wrapper and stick with adhesive tape. Slot it into the slit on one of Robox's hands.

Right . . . **Where is Fidox?**

Make a Code Dial

1. Photocopy this page and cut around the 2 circles.
2. Make 2 holes and place the smaller circle on top of the larger one. Thread a split pin through both circles and into the centre hole on the screen of Computer Control.
3. To make a code: Choose one letter as a 'key', e.g. **E**. Turn the small dial (letters in code), so that **E** is aligned with **A** on the large dial, (letters **not** in code). Keeping both dials in place, read off the rest of the code.

So **HELLO = LIOOS**.

Change your key as you wish.

A Cosmic Circus Comes to Town

Colour cubes

Make 4 cubes following the dice grid on page 58. Place the cubes together so that the colours are not repeated along each of the four rows.

Colour the 4 cubes like this:

1. B / R R B Y / G
2. B / Y Y G B / R
3. G / R B R G / Y
4. Y / R G Y B / Y

Y – yellow G – green
R – red   B – blue

Like this:

Y R G B
R Y B G

An 8-Armed Bandit

You can play a game with the 4 symbols (heart, star, circle, triangle). Draw them on a grid, or on my body, if you make me (see page 75). Position them in the same grid squares as here. Then fill in the missing symbol in every row, across and down.

Ha, ha, hee, Roboxanne looks funny! To make her hat and one for Robox, copy and cut out the patterns on page 73. Then . . .

Answer: page 94

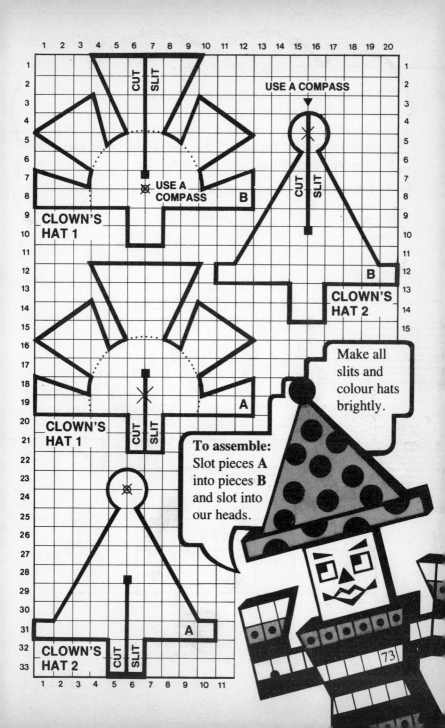

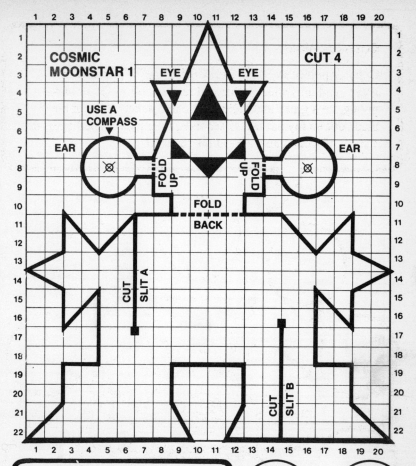

The making of the Moonstars

Copy and cut out this grid and the one on page 76. Make 4 of each (drawing around the first pattern). Draw their faces.

Make all slits and folds.

To assemble Moonstar 1:

1. Slot slit **A** of one piece into slit **B** of one of the 3 other pieces of the Moonstar. Repeat with the 3 other pieces, so he has 4 sides. See page 67.

CONTINUED▶

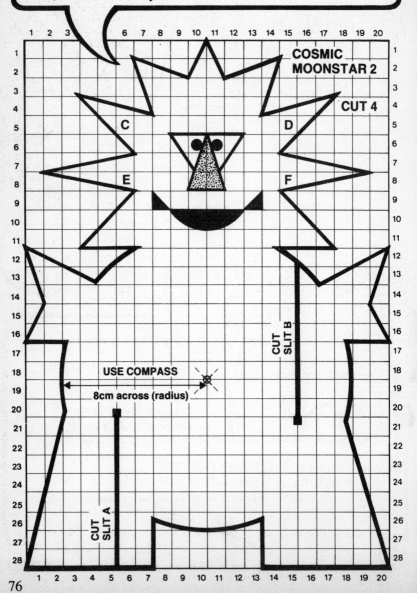

Play Hoopla

Draw and cut out this square, 12cm by 12cm. Cut out the centre square, 8cm by 8cm. Make 2 and stick them together.

Then . . . put Moonstar 1 on the floor. Lie on the floor some distance away, and try to throw your 'hoop' over its head, so that it rests on its ears.

Things to do with the Moonstars

1. Put both Moonstars on the floor and lie on the floor some distance away:

(a) Try to roll marbles through their legs.
(b) Blowing hard, see if you can blow them over!

2. Colour them in bright colours, put on your glasses (page 48) and see how the colours change.

3. Put the Moonstars against a white wall, in the dark. Shine a torch or light on them and cast some frightening shadows.

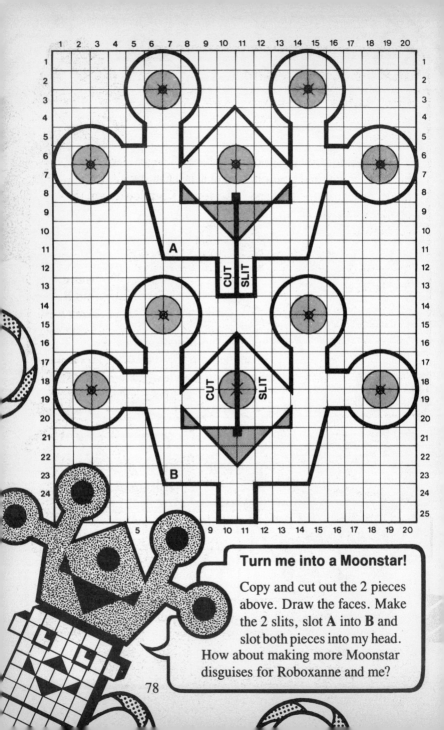

Turn me into a Moonstar!

Copy and cut out the 2 pieces above. Draw the faces. Make the 2 slits, slot **A** into **B** and slot both pieces into my head. How about making more Moonstar disguises for Roboxanne and me?

Meet the Cosmic Conjuror

Count **ALL** the triangles you can see **on** the conjuror and **on** his magic wand. Careful!

To make him, copy the grids on the next 3 pages. Draw in his face, colour and cover him with stars. Cut out all the pieces, make all the slits and folds. Keep looking at the conjuror on page 82 for guidance.

To assemble:
1. The head:
Stick all flaps to the 4 sides but do not stick flaps **1**, **2**, and **3** on the top.

2. The wand:
Slot **A** into **B**. Slot into my hand after making me.

CONTINUED ▶

Answer: page 95

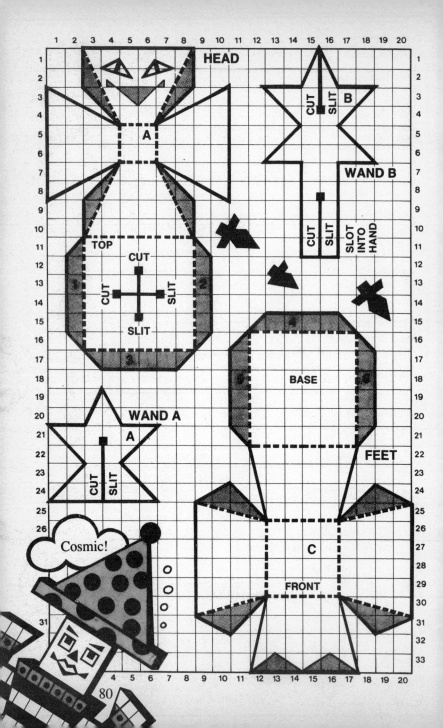

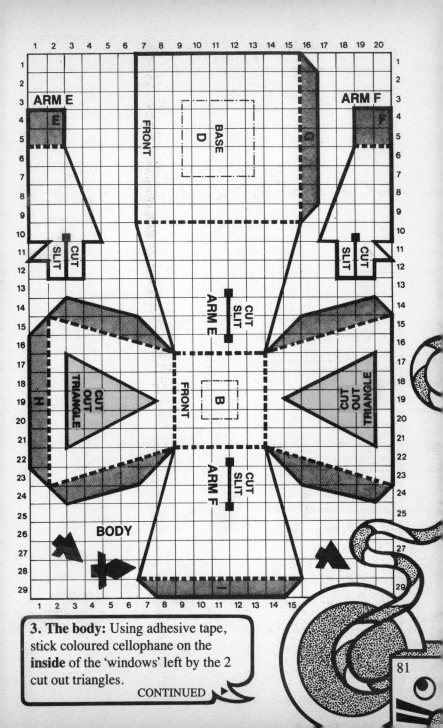

3. The body: Using adhesive tape, stick coloured cellophane on the **inside** of the 'windows' left by the 2 cut out triangles.

CONTINUED

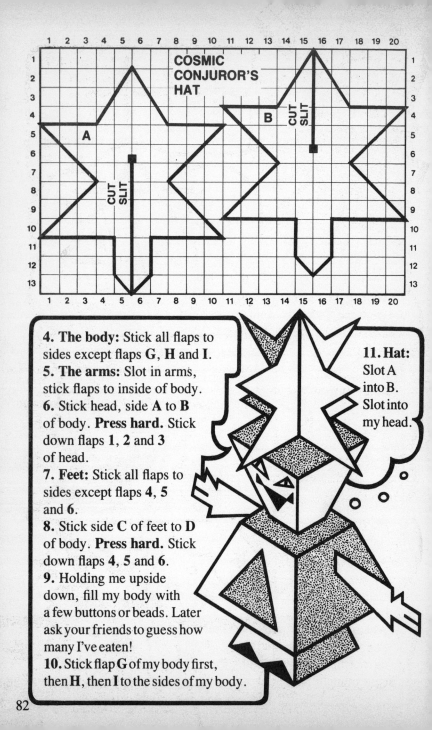

COSMIC CONJUROR'S HAT

4. The body: Stick all flaps to sides except flaps **G**, **H** and **I**.

5. The arms: Slot in arms, stick flaps to inside of body.

6. Stick head, side **A** to **B** of body. **Press hard.** Stick down flaps **1**, **2** and **3** of head.

7. Feet: Stick all flaps to sides except flaps **4**, **5** and **6**.

8. Stick side **C** of feet to **D** of body. **Press hard.** Stick down flaps **4**, **5** and **6**.

9. Holding me upside down, fill my body with a few buttons or beads. Later ask your friends to guess how many I've eaten!

10. Stick flap **G** of my body first, then **H**, then **I** to the sides of my body.

11. Hat: Slot A into B. Slot into my head.

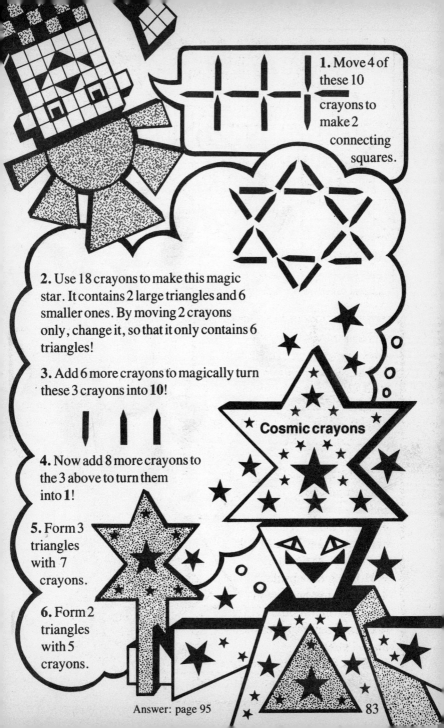

1. Move 4 of these 10 crayons to make 2 connecting squares.

2. Use 18 crayons to make this magic star. It contains 2 large triangles and 6 smaller ones. By moving 2 crayons only, change it, so that it only contains 6 triangles!

3. Add 6 more crayons to magically turn these 3 crayons into **10**!

4. Now add 8 more crayons to the 3 above to turn them into **1**!

5. Form 3 triangles with 7 crayons.

6. Form 2 triangles with 5 crayons.

Answer: page 95

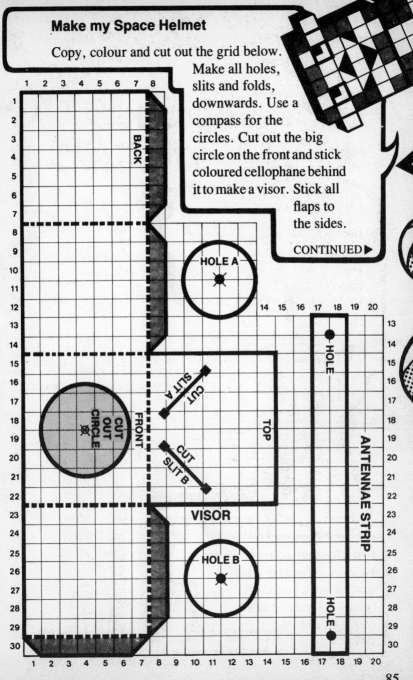

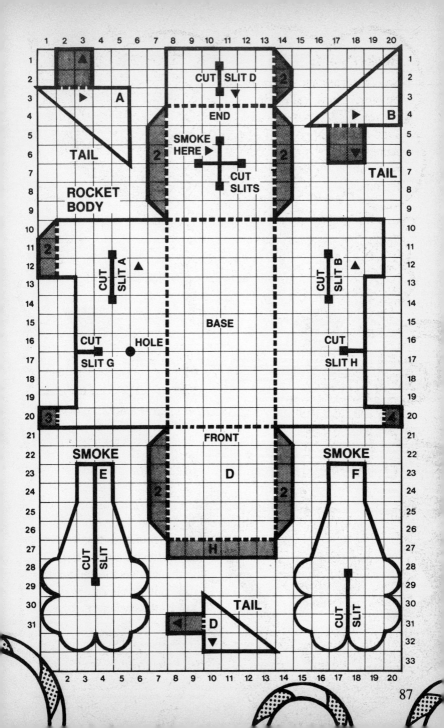

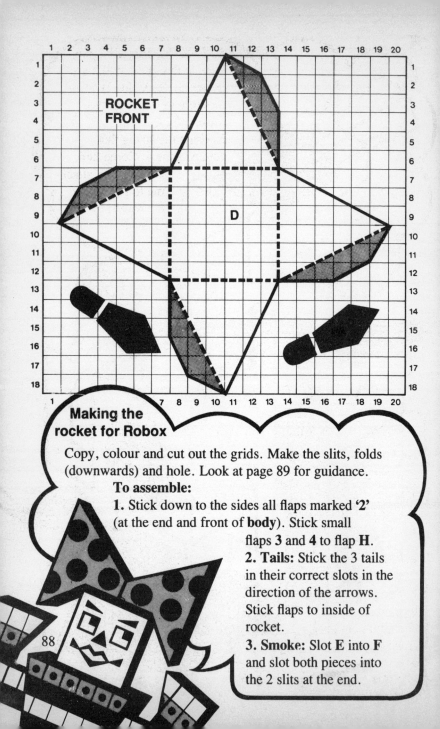

Making the rocket for Robox

Copy, colour and cut out the grids. Make the slits, folds (downwards) and hole. Look at page 89 for guidance.

To assemble:

1. Stick down to the sides all flaps marked '**2**' (at the end and front of **body**). Stick small flaps **3** and **4** to flap **H**.

2. **Tails:** Stick the 3 tails in their correct slots in the direction of the arrows. Stick flaps to inside of rocket.

3. **Smoke:** Slot **E** into **F** and slot both pieces into the 2 slits at the end.

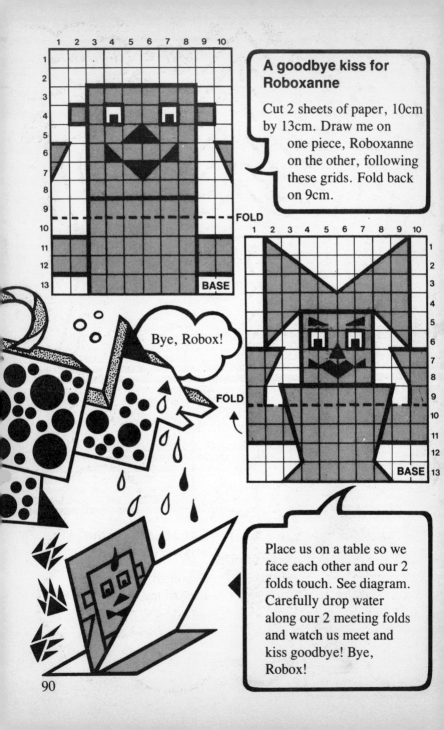

ROBOX FINDS THE ANSWERS

Page 14
Yes, there is a knot in the tail of Mission Mouse!

Page 16
Who am I? I am **ROBOX**!

Page 24
Robox's new friend is called **CHATTERBOX**.

Page 21

M	O	U	S	E	
		T			
		C	A	R	D
B	E	A	R		I
E		T			C
E			O	N	E

Page 27

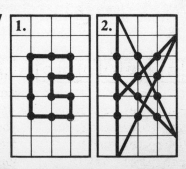

Page 28
1. You can make 72 squares!
3. HELLO, MY NAME IS ROBOX

Page 30
Did you find these 28 words?

BLUE	FOOT	YELLOW	MOUSE
PAPER	CAT	FUN	USE
BIG	CUBE	YES	BOOK
ROBOTS	BOX	DOT	KEY
SWEETS	SAIL	BABY	ROBOX
COMPUTER	SAILOR	STORY	COME
RED	TOY	TALK	DAY

Page 31
Due to a temporary switching of signals to your brain, you should see an 'after-image' of a red **A**, surrounded by a blue background. Did you?

Page 34
CAT-COT-DOT-DOG or
CAT-COT-COG-DOG

Page 36/37
1. CATerpillar 2. CATfish
3. CAT-nap 4. CAT-burglar
Look in the dictionary for more words beginning with **CAT**!

Page 39
Fidox has **63** spots on him!

Page 44

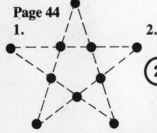

Moves of discs:
1. 4 to touch 5 and 6.
2. 5 to touch 1 and 2.
3. 1 to touch 5 and 4.

Moves of discs:
1. Move 2 and 3 to spaces 9 and 10.
2. Move 5 and 6 to spaces 2 and 3.
3. Move 8 and 9 to spaces 5 and 6.
4. Move 1 and 2 to spaces 8 and 9.

Page 45
Lift this book slowly towards your nose and you will see the lead join up!

Page 48/49
Reflection **B** is the one Robox sees.
Fidox only has **61** spots on him now!

Page 52/53
Roboxanne is **C**.

Page 59
Dice **B** is correct.

Page 62

6	7	2
1	5	9
8	3	4

Page 63
No, there wasn't a knot in Fidox's lead – that is how he ran away!

Now, Fidox has **65** spots on him!

Page 67
The key letter is **B** (bee) and the message reads:
HELLO, ROBOX, I'VE SEEN FIDOX . . . FOLLOW ME AND YOU'LL FIND HIM.

Page 68
The key letter is **T** (tea) and the message reads:
DEAR ROBOX, I'VE GONE TO JOIN THE COSMIC CIRCUS. . . ! BYE, BYE . . . LOVE, FIDOX

Page 71
Roboxanne is holding Fidox's lead.

Page 72

Page 74
Because of a temporary switching of signals to your brain, you should see blue balls against a red (pink) background. Cosmic!

Page 79
There are **66** triangles on the Cosmic Conjuror and on his wand!
This square alone contains **8** triangles!

Page 83
1.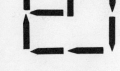
2.
3.
4.

Page 84
The Magic Word is **CHATTERBOX!** Here are just a few words we can make from it. There are lots more!
hate, heat, boat, bear, chatter, robe, broach, tea, beach, roach, cheat, treat, hare, tear, box.